Basic Nest Architecture
Polly Atkin

Seren is the book imprint of
Poetry Wales Press Ltd.
57 Nolton Street, Bridgend, Wales, CF31 3AE
www.serenbooks.com
facebook.com/SerenBooks
twitter@SerenBooks

ISBN: 978-1-78172-373-9
ebook: 978-1-78172-374-6
Kindle: 978-1-78172-375-3

A CIP record for this title is available from the British Library.

The publisher acknowledges the financial assistance of the Welsh Books Council.

Cover Image: © Mary Jo Hoffman, www.stillblog.net.

Printed by 4edge Limited, UK.

Contents

III

I

The individual is nothing, her existence conditional only, and herself, for one indifferent moment, a winged organ of the race. Her whole life is an entire sacrifice to the manifold, everlasting being whereof she forms part. It is strange to note that it was not always so.

— Maurice Maeterlinck, *The Life of the Bee*

Colony Collapse Disorder

When I lived in the city I knew where I was,
what being there was. I knew I breathed
under a film of constant light,
that electricity was life. It moved
in my body, which I knew was an atom of the city,
and kept us twitching in unity. I felt
information bloom in my blood. It sang
in my cells as though it had always been there.
I knew without it I had no structure.

To leave the city was to leave one's memory.
Outside was a garden gone wild. Stars
were night-flowers in a mossy dome, opening
their dazzling mouths to amaze, spreading
exponentially the further from the city I went.
I knew nothing. What nothing meant. I feared
the dark and the space between things: space
needs filling. I'd cry for the city, its order.
To be let back in was to regain the future.

Now I live elsewhere the system is reversed.
The city is a picture from a book I once read
and nothing to do with me. Life is a movement
between dirt and sky. I see this clearly.
The stars are generators. Without them we'd fail.
Going back to the city is to speed myself up
to a drawn out buzz that I know is killing me.
Going anywhere other than elsewhere is rehearsing
this end: the shut-down of travelling energy.

All those years living inside weakened me.
Taken away from elsewhere I dim.
Friends visit and tell me that elsewhere is death
and the sky cannot feed me. Not indefinitely.
Their eyes are blown bulbs. They rattle. I smell
honey on their skin and know how it is.
When they move I hear humming like a swarm at a distance.
When they speak I hear their voices, and under
the city quietly droning.

Buzz Pollination

'Among the humble-bees, for instance,
the workers do not dream of renouncing love.'
               – Maurice Maeterlinck, *The Life of the Bee*

In the mountain orchard this afternoon
I opened my petals to the ripening sun
and the same bee came and came again
to feed at my wrist, tricked by the blossom
of my bracelet's fat fake pearls, their delicious
lustre: peachy, smooth on the tongue.

I'd hear her returning from a distance, her tinnitus
thrum spun in circuits with me at the centre
as though she held onto the hope if she trembled
enough, I'd give something up. She brushed
my skin like a shock, electrostatic.
Her wings stirred the air, whirring, mechanic.

I named her *Hurricane Engine*. My hair
rippled in her storm like long grass. I thought
her soft fuzz would catch on my own and knot us
together. I thought we would learn to speak
as each other. She bumbled, bumbled, but the baubles
did not turn to pollen. They gleamed inorganic.

The shadows slunk longer. I heard her mumble
to the apples. I waited, longed for her, wanting
her powder-puff touch, her yellow, her hunger.

I know her kind. *Bombus*. Her buzz
pollination, that constant dorsal aorta.
Her need for return. The way she will bite
right through a corolla to take its nectar.
The *zizz, bizz bizz!* of her flight muscles, firing.
The reverse-pitch rotary burr of her blades.

She lacks barbs. Stings more than once. Builds simple.
Does not winter well. Marks her sources
as rewarding/unrewarding.

The New Path

'Dr. Thomas Arnold, as progressive in his views on road building as in his politics, used to tease Wordsworth by referring to the picturesque Upper Path as 'Old Corruption', the road over the Common as 'Bit by bit Reform', and the new level road as 'Radical Reform'. Wordsworth was never reconciled to the latter, for the new road cut brutally through Bainriggs wood and destroyed the lonely peace of the lakeshore. We take it nonetheless.' — Grevel Lindop

The new path dislikes colour. It is hard,
like the future. It is grey, like the future. It is made
of similar smaller parts smashed down
to something like stone. The new path means
equality/against disruption, upset.
It cuts your hands when you press on it, testing
to see if it tastes of anything, smells of
living or dead. The new path is cold
on your skin. The new path will flatten everything.
Soon enough you will find yourself chalking
your knees on it, weeping quietly with gratitude
as it scores your palms with its arrow-head brand.
The new path tells us uniformity is perfection.
The new path tells us difference is difficult.
To be difficult is not to be natural. To be limitless
is not to be good. The world is for walking
over, not through. It will teach you to move
without consequence. Without transgressing to dirt
or resistance. The new path leads to nowhere
specific. Is always accessible. Says
    do not try to follow me home.
    I cannot deliver. I am not for travel.
It teaches passivity. Its public name
is Improvement. It will not remember another.
The new path does not like people. The path
is dangerous/does not like danger. The tangled
world is not ready for its definitive stance.
The new path seeps away in the woods
scattering its small grey spores.

Jack Daw

Strut and hop, head cocked. Bill-up posture.
Sky-tumbler. Linear hierarchical order

repeated through faultless falls. Acrobat
soothsayer. Splintered midnight in flight.

College bird, sea crow, chimney-sweep bird.
In French – tower crow – *choucas de tours* –

steeple-jack. In Latin – *Corvus Monedula* –
money crow. Jack of coins. *Jacques d'or.*

Labelled by home or haunt or habit.
Love of the shine. Your bright slick image.

Centuries repeating your own name in greeting
chyak chyak chyak

taught us the sounds
as best as our soft mouths could catch. We parroted

jack. Dubbed you simple – *daw*.
In spring I watch you nest-build, exulting

over sticks; twigs; clumps of tatty wool picked
from barbed wire; moss, human hair, pruning

fleece from a sheep as she sleeps. Any
gap you find you will work on improving.

Day after day I hear you calling
ciao ciao ciao   from the rooftops, tree tops,

chimney pots, edge of the woods   *ciao ciao*
from the village green.   I call you back

*Prince of Smokestack   Chaplin   Inquisitor
of Stars   Moon Eye   Coin-in-a-Well.*

That which you love the best you share
faithfully. Allopreening in pairs.

When you quarrel with yourselves a war is massing
on a distant horizon, a long term forecast.

Thunderclouds flock when you gather, to mimic
your sharp murmurations, to call in the rain.

I know you are trying to tell me something.
I know I could teach you to say it with meaning.

ciao ciao ciao I squawk, signalling
exit/arrival.   A clatter of wings.

I have set a dish of oil in the yard
to catch you with your own reflection.

Your blue-eyed baby is crying in alarm
from the breach in our structure you cracked her into

kae kaya kavka caddy
ka-wattie   caddess   caddow   cawdaw
cathag   jak-y-do   chauk

A short history of the moon

One hundred years after Bartolomeo Christofori built his first
gravicembalo col piano e forte in Padua, Mr. Thomas Moon –
cabinet maker of Plymouth – turned his tools to pianos. Moon pianos.

The heavens have many moons and so did Plymouth: after Father Moon,
Anna Moon, Edward Moon, James Edward Moon, George Winter Moon,
Harold Edward Percy Moon, Captain Sydney Edward Moon,
Lieutenant Harold Rosslyn Moon. Each with an orbit of its own, each
with a gravity tug on the tide. They called
        the shop they kept the House of Moon.

In 1927 a shower of gramophones blazed through the House of Moon,
falling to earth as space dust, galactic rubble, sentient fragments, sprouting
radiograms stuttering phrases from the papers,
        hits from the stars, from the stage.
In 1956 the first small steps were taken on the altered face
of the reborn House of Moon, relayed live to Moon TV, thirteen
years before Armstrong made it. People would rush to visit, sit for hours
in its quiet craters listening to crackly
        galaxies expanding from the Browserie, fractured
reflections tracking their monochrome doubles
        on the screen that echoed them all.

All this time, pianos – Exeter to Exmouth, Barnstaple, Bugle, Truro –
pianos sailing the heaving streets of Cornwall like musical yachts.

In 59 Moon and Sons bought in Pye Transistor radios.
Priced in guineas. Dreams of the future
        imagined in a past replete with pianos.
The pianos in shadow, faces like the full
        toothless moon, that mask of sorrow.
January 1st 1963 Mssrs Moon handed the keys
To Mssrs Stone, Lighting & Radio. Mssrs Stone had no need of pianos.
The moon, of course, was only ever
        stone, its harmonies borrowed from the sun.

I have heard of fragments of moon surviving
                              in living rooms, in far flung places,
salvaged from yard sales, junk piles, storage.
                    Like my magnificent wreck, dredged up
from a Blackpool garage. Or the one the tuner
                    told of, tending the worn-down felt
on my moon's hammers, the only other
                              moon he'd known: a red moon, broken
gutted, planted in the garden of a commune
                    he lived in before I was born, before
he knew to fix her, back in those days
                    when the cool white glow of the House of Moon
might still be caught as a glint in Plymouth's windows on cloudless nights.
You watch me write this through your coppery eyes.

                    I leave the curtains open, hope
a glimpse of the rock you were chipped from long
                    ago, in the age of musicians, lit up
like a beacon, your replicant mirror, will bring
                              a lunar river streaming from your creaking
panels, stripping your peeling varnish,
                    glaze you blue moon, pink moon, all those
years in darkness, locked from the sky, pushed past, a note misplayed. You
shine on, shine on, hold. Sustain.
                    Your brilliance all your own.

Heron/Snow

You carry worlds in the cipher of your feathers;
sky and water woven together

by the black of a wood in winter; blue
grey of the lake, half frozen over:

a dull kind mirror to find yourself in
or to knock on in search of another. Is that

why you waited all morning so patiently, planted
like a post in the field in the snow? There is nothing

here by this road for you, surely, but ground
to launch from, and me, to watch you drawing

your perfect arc in the air, diving
silently upwards into the tumbling

white, as though into a weir. The whole
vale is shaking itself into flakes

and falling, or rising. It's hard to tell.
You in your grace alone remain still

even in motion. I've heard a heron
will attack a human if threatened. I imagine

your beak a spear through my skull, and grasp
at last the beauty of the kill.

Kindling

It was the winter of fires that would not take,
of ash everywhere, never enough heat.
The winter of ice: opaque waves
creeping closer over the roads at night,
shutting you off from time and the outside.
Everything stopped. Your watch, your heater.
You piled all you could on your bed but still
the cold woke you at least twice an hour.
You dozed all morning. Afternoons you prepared
for evening, spent all your daylight kindling,
willing the flames to live; lost hours
crouched in the hearth, giving mouth to mouth
to the sputtering coal, praying for breath.
You knew you were just treating symptoms. The problem
lay farther than you could reach, no matter
how you contorted yourself. The chimney
was stuffed with the stubs of years condensed
into soft black snow that swallowed your stretching
arms when you went to clear it. It needed
more than you had; somebody trained
in removing the past. But this was the winter
you forgot how to use the phone, forgot
how to write a letter, construct a sentence.
You failed in the cold alone, speechless,
convinced it was something you'd done or not done.
By dark the room would be fully ablaze,
lit by laughing flames, denying
there'd ever been a struggle. Meanwhile
months passed, scrunched up like scrap on the grate,
and all that dead weight you ignored built up
like the frost as it kept getting colder.

Stay Apparatus

Out of the travelling window there are always
horses. Dozens in a field by the track
blanketed against autumn mizzle, or flaring
to a bright white blaze on the brow of a hill
by a service station, midsummer, or nuzzling
each other's warm necks in the snow where the limit
switches from forty to fifty, or grazing
the same green triangle month on month.
The more you seek them, the more appear,
as if called out from a hidden field
by a word you were not aware you had spoken
and could not repeat. I was never as awed
as a girl as I am as a woman by horses.
Their lateral vision. Stay apparatus.
Knack for alertness, even in dreams.
How they carry their history so lightly, and seem
not to blame us. A horse kept alone will not sleep
well. A horse kept indoors will sicken.
They are always there, out of every window,
resting, tensing to run.

Roadkill Season

In Eighteenth-Century House it was roadkill
season. Pheasant, hooked out from under
the dented bumper, last breath condensed
in a plastic bag, matured for a week
in the stainless steel back sink, to build up
flavour. Beautiful dead! I never
saw a thing alive so lovely.
The basin, silvered like the lake in winter,
swirled with colour, like dead trees and diesel.
You stank like the kill itself, like the mulchy
scrub you stumbled out of, stupid
and gorgeous, in love with the tarmac. Poorman's
Peacock. Dumb bundle of plumage and flesh.
Laura popped your cooling heart
in her gob like a sweet; burst it between
her sharpening teeth. Kate and Anna
carved your breast to split together.
Your meat was purple as the sky at dusk.
We each hooked a finger to halve your wish-bone,
squeezed our eyes closed, and heaved.
We gathered scraps. Kate buried the shell
to dig up and sculpt into artefact later.
We dried out your feet on radiators.
You clutched hot air as they hardened to stars
we bent into brooches, gifts for each other,
then salvaged the best of your wings and fine tail
and stitched new faces of your feathers.

Miracles of Light

for Ann-Kathrin

Here are the bodies of the warrior saints,
not wasted away, not gone, but sleeping

uncorrupted, dreaming the long
dreams of the blessèd in death. Here

the severed head that reattaches,
limbs taken by birds which turn,

dropped from their beaks like seeds, to living
trees, to streams, to holy water.

Here is the body in fragment, here
the weeping creature, the wolf that carries

the speaking skull, the praying lion,
meek as a griffin, stunned, baptised

by pillars of light in the wild that lead
to the massacred corpse. Light as a beacon,

light as instruction, miracles of light,
the testimony of the beautiful bones' translation,

the healing shrine. Here is the miracle
of murder: by arrows, by clubbing, by goodness

by thrust of lances, spears, beheading,
murder by resurrection. Anointed.

This is your local saint. Oh kingly.
This is your legend of rule. Oh holy.

The monastic–ascetic holy king,
the holy king fallen in battling pagans,

the innocent monarch betrayed. Saints
of edgelands, saints of isthmus and island,

of forested mountain and fell. Arm
yourselves. The hour is coming. May the beams

of your chapel be delivered by stags. May beasts
respect your flesh. May your end be one

for the records. A miracle of light. May your cult
survive, travel further than your bones.

Lake Fever

'He, thus by feverish passion overcome …
Below him, in the bosom of the deep,
Saw mountains'
           – Wordsworth, 'The Brothers'

That moment I was coming home to you
to my blue sky against your green slopes,
blue-green iris of one great eye,
dark wooded pupil.

It was only a photo I pitch-poled into.
It was only the lateness of the hour, the febrile
moths *thup thup* at the double-glazed window
at the back of my skull.

If you were a fever at sea I would dare
those mosses and ferns into ripples, pitching
my whole life into the fiction and wake
mouth full of peaty freshwater, clutching

shards of your inland shore. You don't
believe it? I nearly did it. I was
one foot in and sinking as in
deep black mud. I was hauling up

to dive or let go, and fall.

When I lived alone

When I lived alone I was clean. Good.
I drank jasmine tea in the afternoons
working by lamplight in the gloom. At night
I read by candlelight. Drank Rooibos. Played
piano to the guitar, guitar to the piano.
Sometimes I sang, to them both, to the room,
to myself, alone. Sometimes I went out.
If I left for more than a day I'd stroke
the walls and tell the house to be good
without me. Occasionally, people came round
and made the still, contained air busy.
Mostly though it was only me,
me and the house, being good together.
I slept curled up against the cool
stretch of its ribs like a cub. It breathed
gently into me. How I loved
its scent of damp sandstone and old warm
wood. I loved how it touched on my mind
and shifted its light to my mood. How
it helped me be good. In the mornings I'd sit
in its eye with a pot of good black coffee,
reheating it on the hob as it cooled.

Sister, Running

for E.P.

Hurricane came calling last night, singing warnings,
and you, little sister, you'd let yourself out
to howl at the swooping clouds till they split
and spat pellets of stars. The trees would not dance
as you wanted. The mountains kept forcing you back.

You screeched in each wheezing chimney, shrieked
as each road sign whined in disharmony, thrumming
your nails on slates

staccato

glissando

Nobody slept.   Everyone dreamt.

Your tears became blades in the earth, sprouting.

This morning a tree barred your door, mouthing
lines you thought you'd shed: *he is thin
in his ends.* The fells are in sun. Climb over
the fallen, kick off, keep running.

Rabbit in morning

When I wake in the morning you are waiting for me,
sat in the yard, still as a tree stump,
only your eyes and nostrils moving,

and the wind in your fur, and the rushing shadow
of leaves crashing over your curve, a green
sea of waves on shingle, combing

your sandy flanks, your reddish back.
After a pause, sure you are watched,
you stretch out into a living leap

and plunge in the pool of long cool grass.
This is the reason I won't cut the lawn:
to see you so, only ears above water

then arcing over like a dolphin saluting
the sun, playing in the wake of the house
as it sails me on, for sheer pleasure

of throwing yourself up. I want to invite you
in, or to stay, or to not go away,
but you are a wild thing. All I can do

is believe you will keep on being the warm
vaulting life, ravelled round mine,
although I may never hold you.

Athena Glaukopis

I meant for a blackbird. It cried all day
from the weeping birch. I don't know why
I had to show you. The moving leaves

muddled our shadows. Instead of the merl,
an owl, tall and brown, stretched
to the trunk. I pointed, but you would not see.

Not even when it unlocked its deep
eyes. Met mine. No, for you,
only its wings and belly, pale

as the afternoon moon as it flew. We squinted
at treetops in sun, holding hands.
A bus groaned past. The blackbird sang.

All night, those black eyes staring. A gift
or a message. Opening and opening.

Illustrations of Grasmere Church

Potnia Theron

Our lady of animals, was it you in the meadow
in the mist where the calves grazed by starlight, their breath
white globes in the dark? We stopped dead, sensing
shadow shifting, our own breath pooling
into phosphorous moons, feeling the deep
hush of invisible hooves, drifting
over the tips of the blades of the grass
as though skating on dew. When the first stag raised
its head and its antlers were moonlight, we knew.

Now every evening the freezing cloud skulks
from the peaks, we listen for the quiet of their feet,
to find you shivering on the drive in the shape
of a hind. Inside, we expect the glow
of your eyes at the black of the window, your furred
face emerging from the field of fog,
the glass between us. To want you is dangerous.
To forget you, worse. Mistress of wilderness.
In the old tongue, there were only chattels and Dēor.

Waking the Well

It spills itself on tarmac, dressed
                               in weeds. Thinks itself forgotten.
Disproven hydropathic quack.
                               A cross on an antique map. Archived.
Machinery broken up in museums.

It belongs to May. Sugar-water
                               Sundays crazed with growth, stone
blessed till it ruptured colour, sweet
                               spring ringing out with the bluebell scent
of long light health, cool wonder.

Before the last I will kneel on the damp
                               grass at its feet, bare-legged, hands
open on knees, palms up – blank
                               mirrors to a surge of sky – drink
in silence. Lick open its liquorice eyes.

Rise.   Walk on into the lake.
                               Trust the water to matter.

A history of flooding

Everyone knows it, the system is broken.
We knew when we took this place on it came
with a history. February last, that night
the main road filled to the thighs just north
of the village sign, they went to sleep
with it seeping in under the doors, woke
to an inch all over like a chemical dip.

There's a house, we're told, where they used to lift
the floorboards, watch as the waters rose.
Below our living room carpet, concrete
shrouds the ghosts of bowing beams
and the village dead crouched down to take
the measure of the murky surge, the boards
a raft, the cottage a heavy float.

The field is a lake again, the lake
a bucket spilling over in rain. The river
will not stick long to its channel. It charges
its margins, testing its run up, its bolt.
The road out, both directions, sinking.
And under the floorboards at the end of the row
the flood, unobserved, rising.

II

And I awoke in struggles, and cried aloud — 'I will sleep no more!'
— Thomas De Quincey, *Confessions of an English Opium Eater*

In the city I was born in

In the city I was born in it snows all day
but shows nothing of it. Its pavements smudge
or stain as with rain, or are pressed under ice,
smooth and opaque after weeks of compression,
smattered with towndirt like shot. A thin wind
snaps round its sharp-cornered streets. People
fall where they stand. The snow is fast
and light. Insistent. I've travelled inland
as far I can but no sign can come
and now I am stuck. City I was born in,
you should know I've not come here to die,
but not unlike it: to stop for a while.

Somewhere a body like mine is lying
in a bed of its own, in a house of its own,
which blue drifts smooth to a glacial barrow
while ice builds urgent weight at its windows
and stars plummet down on threads like spiders
to light the dreamer's gaping mouth.
Can you honestly say I belong to you, city
that refuses to comply with the national weather,
sole grey smear on a whited-out map?
You are not my end point, barely my home.
I'm a spider tumbling into your yawn.
I see you are more afraid than I am.

Your grey day is dimming. The man I love
stands at his door looking into your shadows
and says without turning *something is falling,*
something is falling, but nothing settles.

Moon Salutation

This is what you came home for, you
and the mountain and the forest and the stars in the dark

and the moon, half a blink from full,
low, white and cool as the eye

of a jackdaw in the feathered night. You move
slowly at first, where the trees block the light.

The wood expands, contracts you down
the gallery of its ribs. Your breath is a tight

hiss in your ears, strange as the voices
you catch spilling up from the village, mixed

with hoots of an owl, the crunch of boots
on leafmeal and gravel. The open is silvered,

fixed in reverse – a daguerreotype portrait.
You stop at each curve of the path and stare.

The valleys drown under floods of fluorescing
cloud. The high ground glints and shifts.

Noises rise like sounds above surface
heard under water, distorted – a shout –

a motorbike's revs as the church clock strikes
midnight. You count the chimes, climb

far out at sea, dreaming land
from the ghost of a ship's bell tolling. Scared

of falling, but more of sinking. You keep
pushing uphill. Your bare arms shine

like armour. You are a crescent, waxing.
A few feet further, half an hour longer,

and you'll be complete: a perfect mirror,
spheroid and luminous, reflecting everything,

unable to go back, ever.

Strength in Winter

February. The lion, rising in the east
            with its bright motor, *Cor Leonis*, pulsing.
We catch sight of it one night through a wound in the cloud.
We are the dead light travelling and the bodies on which it falls. Gravity
                        darkens us. We are on the brink
of spinning apart, no matter to burn. It is too cold for strength in winter.
We are scattering out of our orbits as dust.
We have lost clear sight of ourselves as more
than meat and water. The lion stretches its limbs, limps over Jupiter, yawns.
The heart of the lion is blue and strong. 134 x more radiant than our sun.
Qalb al-Asad, Regulus, Basiliscus, Nakshatra Magha the bountiful, Rex,
the star who stands at the lion's breast.
                        So much of us they have put a name to.
            Alpha to Chi Leonis. 1-95 Leonis.
Beta Leonis is Denebola – *Deneb Alased* – *Al Ṣarfah*, the Changer –
the lion's tail, switching the skies. Delta is *Zozma, Zosca, Zubra,*
Dhur – the girdle, the flank. Theta is *Chertan, Chort, Coxa* – the small
ribs and the hip. Omicron, *Subra*, the paw and the unseen thorn in its pad.
Epsilon is *Ras Elased Australis, Algenubi*, the southern crest
of the mane, to mirror Mu Leonis, *Ras Elased Borealis,*
Alshemali, the northernmost hair, and Zeta Leonis, *Adhafara,*
forelock, kiss-curl of inviolable fur, fringing the limits of Gamma Leonis,
Algeiba, Juba, the forehead's lintel over Kappa, *Minkhir al-Asad*, the muzzle,
the gleaming jaw which – Lamda, *Alterf* – swallowed the beast's own eye.
We must learn to speak of what we are made of –
            deep sky objects, spiral forms,
circumstellar debris, runaway stars – lunar mansions of oracle bones.
            Phi Leonis. Xi Leonis. Pi Leonis. Tau Leonis, Wolf 359.
                        Only then will we leap up dancing.
In April we will open our doors to mountains,
                our troubles revealed as the splinters they are.
Obsolete galaxies' luminous ghosts stuck in our chests. The sickle in Leo –
that question reversed – pulls them free, one curved cut. We stand at dusk
on the wooded howe and watch them rising
                        over the crown of the boulders they call
            The Lion and Lamb – the known and unknown
elements of our prowling bodies unfolding
                from the blooming sky – our earthly asterisms,
                        our pantherine natures, our terrible pride.

Moving

When it rains heavily water leaks in
through the vent of the extractor fan. You put

a pan on the hob before you lock up.
It is raining heavily   drip   drip
drip. The pan is too small. You imagine it

filling, full, then spilling over
over the night, the kitchen aflood,
water cascading out of its ill-sealed
box. You, arriving back

in the dark of the following evening to find
your home a river, your precious possessions
stolen, drenched downstream or sunk
deep into mud, ruined or lost:
all the photographs you just piled on the shelves

of lives you barely remember, washed clear
like the levee of old leaves drifting around
the house, their shifting mounds, and how
you meant to clear them but now will not need to.

On the train you watch the storm through the window
redefine the sky and landscape you move through
not sure anymore if this is a fear

or a lightness of self
you aspire to.

Dreams

You are sick to death of my dreams.
I drag them out, one after another,
determined to air them as though that could make them
better. They harden in the sudden oxygen
like polythene spooled from a beaker, no longer
integral, robbed of fluidity. No wonder
they seem to tighten around you, snapping
unnatural teeth that scatter about you.
I'd take them back but they do not know me
now they are out. They've moved beyond me.

Weeks later they're still turning up. You find them
covered in dust, lurking in corners
or stuck to the underside of a cup,
or your shoe, or marooned in the tub, strange spiders.
I'd say I was sorry but you'd know I was lying.
They've followed me round this way for years
and I'm tired of trying to wash them down,
or catch them under an upturned glass,
avoiding their creep on my skin. They think
they are yours now. They are. You let them in.

Tiny Glass Horses

Half caught in the watery corner of one
wandering eye. Feral. Prancing
over the frozen field with a tinkling
rattle of silver bells like dripping
icicles dropping one after one
from a cornice thick with late spring snow.
Arpeggio of miniature hooves chipping
music from the austere ground as if digging
for food in an hunkering season. *Chink
chink.* Are they dancing or harrowing? Now
flaring their crystalline nostrils at vitreous
sky, throwing their heads back *chink*
thrashing manes smashed to shards
of clattering ice on their necks. *Chink
chink.* Pellucid bodies weighty
as icebergs. Sailing through thick white sea.
Chink. Terrible harmony. Trick
of the screen. Clouds too breaking themselves
on their own brittle flanks. Surely an error.
Chink. Innumerable marble eyes staring
straight into mine through the glass.

Rabbit in Twilight

It's the boundless dispersal of light that lets us
exist co-synchronous, calmly, anxiety
ticking away like the last of the day

taking all barriers with it. We spill
out from our skins and into everything;
everything into our skins. You are

every rabbit now although
I know you are many: the one breathing hard
in the grass on the verge of a motorway junction,

or waiting to cross a farm road, squeezing
under a fence, displaying only
the dancing white flash of you leaving me, leaving,

or quietly breaking down the garden
mouthful by mouthful, or forming a statue
of yourself by the stable-door. Neither of us

makes any sound at all but the voiceless
noise of living, limitless, both
ourselves more than ever, completely each other,

each other's creatures. We flood with night
and I am every woman you've ever
run from, startled at, moved alongside.

Other People Dream of Foxes

Because you told me briefly, leaving
out details, both of us far from home,

the version that haunts me is set in the house
I grew up in, meaning the fox your dream killed

was our own garden fox, the one we watched
lounging on the roof of the shed like a lion

surveying his dominion, gracious and unlikely,
striding straight out of our jumbled vision

to stretch himself out in the sun. It was
his unmistakable features I saw

peering over the back of the rococo chair
as though he had crept in to curl by the fire

as you sat, sleepy with winter, you
and my sister-in-law. In this scene it is Christmas,

the room full of candles and looking-glass baubles,
the fox-pelt staring with glassy eyes,

tail on the carpet like rusty tinsel.
Perhaps it's a catchlight that makes you start

and realise the danger, the creatures dancing
in its pupils, giving off sparks. Sister-

in-law says *you better get rid of it, quickly*
and so you do, taking your lead

from a story you said you'd forgotten but must
have remembered: the friend of my brother's who boiled

a fox's head to the skull in their shared
student flat. Left too long

the bones dissolved to a thick grey soup.
No time to lose, you dash to the kitchen,

cram the fox-fur into a pan
and set about stewing it down to nothing:

those things in its eyes must be stopped! Imagine
the damage they'd do. Imagine. It's not

this that I see when I picture it: you
steering a great wooden spoon round a cauldron,

but the look on the fox's face as he rests
his muzzle on the golden brocade, still smiling,

amused to find himself finally invited
to dinner in his neighbours' den.

2.

Most girls make wolves into monsters. For you
it was always foxes: one more thing

we could never agree on, for all that sharing,
sprawled on our stomachs on the lawn, swinging

our legs like we were still children, or lying
in bed awake, whispering to the dark

things we might never admit by day.
That's when you told me your nightmare: fluid

foxes pouring through the keyholes of doors
you'd locked to keep them out, streaming

one after another after another, lips
curled the better to show their teeth,

a constant flow of incisors, dripping
with hunger, impossible to push back as water.

You were drowning in foxes. You woke up gasping,
and never shook off the fear of sinking

under the swell of fur. So vivid
it could have been me underneath it. Some days

I've woken bristling in half-dark, stinking
of fox, and thought it was.

3.

Stood on the station platform you squint
into the clear white light. Snow

low on the fells and the sky as blue
as your own side-lit eyes. Your chest hurts. Yesterday

frost so dense it held all day
against the sun, ice in the dips

of the path through the woods like annealed glass, thick
and clouded. Later you lay semi-supine

on the old road amazed at the stars. Cracked
tarmac cold through your coat, frosted

grass crackling at your hands. To the west
of Orion's belt you saw them, pink tongues

lolling as you let them pass. Now
here they are at the station, in place

of your train, shaking snow from their coats,
ghosting across the tracks.

4.

Through the computer you told me last night
I forced you to walk to the west of the lake

to collect the carcass of a fox from the beach
and drag it back in an old plastic bag.

It was heavy as a wet wool coat. It stank.
It left a trail of itself in your place.

You hated it, hated its weight. The sense
of light feet stalking your steps, on scent.

Doll Parts

In the night I had twins.   They came out alright,
but soon they were dying   while I was pursuing
something that wasn't important enough
to turn children to nothing.   My twins were dolls
with their arms ripped off   exposing dark sockets.
I thought about tearing the arms from some other
dolls to save mine.   I could not do it,
and knew then and there I had failed as a mother,
staring into the open drawer
of babies/barbies   unable to make
a decision on which smooth plastic parts
would fit   which owner   like me   would not miss them
until far too late.   I did not take them.
Gnashing my teeth over dolls piled deep
as a plague-grave I knew   I could never remake them.
Only the ones I had born could be sure
to have life in them   bones to be broken.

Perihelion

It spins on this. The barely perceptible
        distinction between a scaled ellipsis
and a perfect circle. The closest we will get

all year and all you show of yourself
        is a backlit cloud, a blimp of luminous
peach, haltered to gloamy grey

by which to hold things. Not one ray scuffed
        this valley floor all day. Beneath
my blanket I sicken in the gloom. Even

if you'd shown, you'd have passed the bar
        of the western mountain horizon before
I'd practised putting outdoor clothes on.

A year will pass in which you shrink
        from me then shiver back.
I'll know you as well from that further distance.

More genuine then. I will sweat in your glare.
        Technically it's not the space between
but the angle that makes the difference.

Dreaming the Organ

i.m. Nellie Taylor d. June 27th 1918

From the organ's beating walls sprout
26 speaking stops – smooth
ivory nodes, stubs of long bones,
each one stamped with the name of the rank
it controls, in small black capitals
                              TROMBA
                    FLUTE HARMONIC
            OPEN DIAPASON
Speaking stops, articulate sound
unplugging the mouths of the old dead under
the floor's heavy stone, a complex geology
of earth and text, discordant history.
Twenty-six, one for each letter,
each note your dream wants to type, each label
a code in a tonal alphabet, each
gasp a word without language, melodic
orthography
            TREMULANT
                    DULCIANA
                                VOX ANGELICA
                    SALICET
            CHOIR
drawn from double-bleached keys, ebony
sharps, soundboards of straight-grained mahogany,
native pitch as the sounding length
of faith. *Lift eyes unto the hills.*
THIS ORGAN | THE GIFT OF SORROWING | PARENTS
elegant engine of meaning
                        SWELL
the only means to make work that might breathe.

Gloria

The hounds pawing, pawing the ground.
                                    – Gloria Anzaldua, 'Cervicide'

Gloria, today my poem came true.
I thought of you, of the slaying of the tame
self to save the group. This morning
I opened the door to a young deer quivering
by the car just like I wrote. The self
out? a god? neither? I tried
of course to follow when it sprang, scanning
the sodden moss for the print of its hooves,
but it vanished by the swollen river, left
no mark as proof. All week the wind
playing the house like an ocarina
and the floods rising, drawing the wild things
down from the woods. Each day misted,
barely light.
                    Gloria.
                              Deer!
I yelled to the man inside who saw it,
not as I did on the drive, it was gone
already, but in his mind: the deer
he dreamt the previous night. Live.
Leaping. This evening, the whole silvered herd
running at the long night moon.

Sky, falling

In the eaves of the ceiling above my bed
a hole is becoming. A web in negative
spinning itself. We're done with spiders;
there's only me here and scuttling matter.
Cracks fork out in the plaster like lightning,
a spiral of emptiness, pressing the air
into sheets and pushing. The outside is trying
to bore through my casing and let itself in.
It will win, no question. It's there in the pattern:
white split by black into segments, spokes
of a wheel which will roll down into me, whether
I choose it or not. It will move. It will move me.
It grows, a rose window. Blooming, it makes
this up-turned ship of a room, a cathedral.
It widens like an eye to the sky. It cries

build your telescope now and be ready. The stars
are weighty. The planets grow heavy. This attic's
the skull of your wood and slate body. This hole
is your mind's observatory. Allowing it scope
is affording enlightenment. Space will drain in
as water drawn into a plughole, your soul
will swell like a seed in the rain, fat
with potential. Think how the spheres will peer in
as you sleep, and your dreams, so human and small
will meet their cold beams as they fall and enlarge
in their light fields to something immeasurable. It's almost
inevitable. All it requires is time
and the courage to give in to gravity, strength
to do nothing. Look! Even now the lid opens.
Lie back, and watch the sky falling.

Solstitial

We are drawn by a map of sweet ash winding
through the twilit streets. There should be three fires:
one of clean bones, one wood, one both.

We have only split logs and white wax to offer
and a tithe of furred moths, and a swan's egg washed
to the shore in a flood, two days earlier.

We pass the sloshing oval from palm
to palm, cold as stone, full
of things that will not happen. We float

wreaths from the candle-lit jetty to the dark
fretful heart of deepest water;
bunches of foxgloves and elderflowers;

give ourselves to the lake to slake
the calamitous storms of the future; muttering
moonshine, mid-mid, most inclined,

axial tilt. We drink. We burn
the sickly half-year, leap the flames
solemn, hallooing. Our voices spin

round the dish of the vale, which is also a crater,
which is also a wheel. We want to sing
through the centre but the night is too light here, cloud

confusing the jagged horizon. We try
to feel it. 23.09. Maximum
cant. The exactness anachronistic.

Mid-mid most-inclined we chant
like a hymn or something older.
We will wash our faces with cold grey dew.

We will sleep with flowers pressed under our pillows.
We will run the streets naked at three in the morning,
the sun almost starting to rise.

III

Immensity is within ourselves. It is attached to a sort of expansion of being that life curbs and caution arrests, but which starts again when we are alone. As soon as we become motionless, we are elsewhere; we are dreaming in a world that is immense.
— Gaston Bachelard, *The Poetics of Space*

Begin

It comes as a flashback of film you excised
from the final release. You're barely sixteen,

watching these doctors with ticker-tape tongues
spewing out corkscrews of letters, like words

except with no meaning. Look, how you hook
them out of your mother's red handbag, biting

fear back, catching them, scrunching them up
and feeding them into your jean back-pocket

to save for the bluetime when everyone sleeps,
humming like fridges in midnight kitchens,

and you are alone, alive in the ticking
bomb of the nighthouse. Then you play

medical snap with the encyclopaedia
trying to match up your blood with its names

what a game! But you don't remember. It
never happened: you did, still do. You lived

and now it appears those night excursions,
lit through a filter of wavery moon,

were dreams. You know you always did
remember your dreams, confuse your dreaming

world with life. Now, shake out your limbs.
This is it: stand up, wake up. Begin.

The Centre

I came back because my heart was sick
with wandering. Because the painted world
was a backdrop from a dream of a show, dimensions
all wrong, perspectiveless, tasting of nothing.
I could not go on with such longing – that constant
twitch of the cellular compass, cutting
my throat every time the bar swung, metronome
ticking *come home come home come home*

but this is a place where children die,
where faith is erased like mountains in rain
or radio waves, where the body ails,
drowning in air, whittling down
to bone, purified, burnishing. O
how we shine in the sharp blue glare of the moon!
We are gods when we walk on the clouds. We are mountains
in rain. Search, and you will not find us.

Your blood knows the heart-place, better than geography.
The path is unmapped at your feet. One sleep
as its guest is a lifetime displaced. Take
no food, no drink, no gift.

Rabbit in hiding

How small you are today, how young.
Young enough to judge it safe
to come this close to my doorway, in search
of something good to eat. I rest
my aching forehead on the glass panel
in the kitchen door and watch. You're scraggy,
thin. You've been out in the rain. Something
I do not realise I do spooks you.

Instead of running you turn your back
to show your tail and turn to stone,
blending yourself with the pebbles, dipping
your head so your ears disappear, your shaking
body bunched in a sphere. Your spasming
heart ripples your fur. The glass
is cool on my skin. I'm crying and now
I can't tell your browns and greys from gravel.

I step back. You're no longer a rabbit
but a rock over which I will stumble.

Cannulation

So much a pen, that night you dream
                              you write with it, invisible ink,
the nib always running dry, your hand
                              unsteady. To start, you pull it out
of the crook of your elbow where it's sat
                              a token of a broken wing, the barbs
of the quill stripped bare
                    to the point it pierces
                              skin, the tip in air, all feather.
In truth it is writing in you, one
                    same fraction of one same letter over
and over, the prickling dot of an I
                    your ticking mind calls tittle – for intra
venous perhaps – but also the child
                    of the long hollow reed I, I, I,
the self made small, importing little
                    one jot
                              iot
                                   iota
                                        drip.
By dawn your forearm is fat with it
                    your silent indecipherable truths pooled
          together in your swelling wrist.

Causeway

Crossing over you panicked I'd drive us
under. I doubted myself, the clock,

the water. The sun was yellow and long.
I'd got us lost already, looking

for somewhere to stop. Now we wavered,
counting out-loud by a tide-table facing

moonish sands, warning signs:
causeway spotted with seaweed, sea-lochs

in miniature, mirroring epic sky.
You gripped the passenger doorhandle, eyeing

the shifting horizon. I can't say for certain
we left the island wholer. We put

our feet in the earth, climbed a bank
of long stiff grass. Photographed each other.

For half an hour we breathed in light
then chased inland, though the road was dry,

passing again the white wooden tower
that looked to us like war, but stands

to hold up life. *Healing island.*
We do not know what it means. They say

nobody knows what it means.

Imaging

We can't say for certain how long it had been there
before we found it, masked by the hulk
of the wardrobe, our own poor perception, its creeping
rapidity, the weak radiation of winter
light — its circular messages breaching
the paper that glossed its scribblings over
so many blinkered moons. It lived
in our midst, clandestine. We slept together.
It breathed in the cavities of our dreams.

Scanned in the ray of the torch, the flash
of the camera, it was there then everywhere, catching
from its image — bruiseish weals erupting
in thorns, furling around the skirting,
enforcing its dominant logic — proliferating
code consuming the walls, the ceiling.
No way to stem it. Sporing from my tremulous
body. It meant us ill. Today
lain on my back on the motorized table,

I met its whorling motion in the dark
sinus revealed by the whirring wheels
with each clicking cycle I held my breath through.
                Someone is already reconstructing me
                        slice by slice with it inside.
Nothing makes sense without contrast. I turned
my eyes from the beam while they fed me in
the doughnut ring — like the mouth of a black
hole — and we stretched out forever.

Fog/Fox

Awake in pain, 4am, I creak
downstairs for a glass of water, a break

from the effort of sleep, and find the window
replaced with a field of pixilate grey,

the tv-screen of the small hours of childhood,
no signal coming, no message but nothing.

Fog on the move, advancing, taking
the ghost trees wavering at the seen world's fringes,

and now the river, and now the walls,
the fells long gone, the homes, the farms

pebbles in the placeless belly of the blank.
I feel their weight though I no longer think them,

I feel their tap-roots tug in the burrow
under the concrete under the carpet

under my feet. I watch Fog swallow
metre by metre the reliable matter

I thought I had figured. I make a pact
to wait till the pale mass touches glass

then go if I can. Inches before
it closes the gap, Fox lopes in

solid and bright in her frame, mouth wide,
warm tongue feeling her way. One of us

walks off, one of us fades.   You must not
blame her. You would do the same. You would stalk

with your gums drawn back, teeth sharpened. She must take
what her body can hold, or be taken.

The Glorious Fellowship of Migraineurs

When we gather we greet each other
by lifting tentatively one hand to one eye.
We meet in darkened rooms, quietly;
share no wine. Nobody speaks
but often our voices join to moan
the migraineurs psalm, low and holy.

The hours before fizz brilliantly, scented
with burnt toast and oranges, petrol, sparking
fireworks, fireflies, stars. Everyone
dons a halo, everyone's soul
shines out through their pores, whether unnaturally
small or wrapped in a skin of water.

We sleep the night together, slip off
one by one on waking from
a dream we pass between us, in which
the structure of the sky is revealed. We make
no dates, but palm to temple, salute
in a migraineur's kiss, our transcendence.

Free Night

The stable doors are locked and crossed.
The stable doors are sealed and veiled:

sprigs of ash, juniper, hawthorn,
whitethorn, elder, rowan.

On every fell great fires are lit.
Flames singe the hem of the rising moon.

We are full with a species of madness. We brim.
Our bones are the flints we strike together.

We will scorch our sick selves off, turn
weakness to ash. A long time ago

we were saints or gods. Healing oil trickled
from the joints of our bones. We rode on the backs

of clouds like storms were our horses, swathed
in the slick skin of swans. Wish girls, we spoke

with the birds, we answered to no one, no one.
Now we stand in the middle of the road,

in the middle of the night, brittle and human,
tarmac cold through our old thin soles,

numberless stars all shrieking at once.
We throw our hands up, heads back, earthly,

mundane with want. The longer we stare
the more of their tumbling sparks appear:

a bee-dance of matter we cannot interpret.
We have fallen too far from flight. Solid

with mud and blood. Our feet are freezing,
our faces, numb. Tomorrow is Spring.

Tonight we set fire to it all.
Our bones the flints we strike together.

We will whistle our wishes down their long hollow cores.
We will slit the membranes of our tight-skinned shadows.

Tonight we are full with a species of madness.
Tonight we set fire to it all.

The Test

For the test, you are always alone.
            You are always cold, naked under
a borrowed gown, your skin a sallow
            mirror to corridor walls. The light,
metal, tinny on the tip of your tongue.
            They shunt you from window to screen, from chair
to bed, from trolley to tipping table.
            The test always happens shut in, no sky,
in a room like a cell with no break in the panels.
            You remember your name like string, balled up
with your clothes your phone your outdoor shoes.
            You have left them behind, folded in a plastic
shopping basket. For the test you must be
            empty. Absented. You signed the forms.
You took what they gave and agreed to their terms.
            This repeats. You are cold. Always alone.
At last, the curtain is drawn on your turn.
            As instructed, you calmly climb in and lie down.
The test does not hurt. The test is not dangerous.
            The test won't take long. As soon as you can
you are free to go home. You are pliant and dumb
            even with the probe at your throat, your right leg
kicking and the vomit rising. You thrash
            enough enough but no one is listening.
At the end you are told you have passed. The notes read
            responded well to the test.

With Feathers

'Let's talk about the beehive of the heart/the cuddy duck of the heart/The heart's Cuthbert'
— Gillian Allnutt

No one needs another poem about the heart as a bird *flap*
flap in a cage of cartilage and bone. Trapped. A flutter not quite tachycardia
but on the way there. They must be small,
     these birdhearts the poets write of, light
and ineffectual as wrens or angels. No one would want a goshawkheart
a cormorantheart a heronheart the ludicrous stretch of an albatrossheart
tearing a horizon from the membranes within
     or the serrated fringes of an owlheart, silently
shredding the chest wall, hacking up pellets
into the abdominal cavities. No one
writes of the beak or the talons. No one writes of what it feeds on; shit
     as sediment, solidifying the diaphragm.
The eggheart: the thing within, a bomb.
No one writes of the noise at night.

The Canon of Proportions

★

You are constantly shifting between sixteen positions. We call this
'the fidget sign'. We know what a regular action should look like
and this is not it. We are checking for variance. For abject difference.
This process may hurt. Look at your hands, they are ripe with blood
your body is failing to move where it should. Why are you trying
to speak when we've shown your mouth is too narrow
                                        too crowded with anomaly?

It is not for us to judge, but to measure. Divinity lies
not in the parts, but the arrangement of parts. Relativity is god.
This is the doctrine of the mean. The golden cut. All
that is good. Proper. And you, with your variant figures, your
gibbon limbs, spider digits, your body a disaster
collage, patched in the dark, like a thing from fiction, what
                                        is your kind if not non-human?

★

from the hairline to the bottom of the chin
                is one-tenth of the height of a man
from below the chin to the top of the head
                is one-eighth of the height of a man
from above the chest to the top of the head
                is one-sixth of the height of a man
from above the chest to the hairline
                is one-seventh of the height of a man
the length of the hand of a man
                equals one-tenth of the height of a man
and the length of the outspread arms
                is equal to the height of a man.

the maximum width of the shoulders –
                a quarter of the height of a man,
from the breasts to the top of the head –
                a quarter of the height of a man,
from the elbow to the tip of the hand –
                a quarter of the height of a man
from below the foot to below the knee –
                a quarter of the height of a man,
from below the knee to the root of the penis –
                a quarter of the height of a man
and the length of the outspread arms –
                equal to the height of a man.

                        ★

No penis by which to gauge the distemper of your halves.
Four cubits make a man. A man is 24 palms.
No order for a creature so uneven. Outside history
and reasonable criterion, you stretch unequal to your own strange span.
These primordial arms. These ridiculous hands. You've lived with them
generations. Now you see their nature – recondite deviants –

how they scratch and tear at the canon of proportions, its splendid logic.
How your body, incalculable sum of its parts, stands as revolt
wholly against the notion of ratio. Mutant. So
obvious, once you address the right section. The reckoning remaining –
what parcel of your flesh is it we count too large/
                                too small ?

The Invisible

'The secret is to walk evading nothing'
        – Alice Oswald

Croneshadow stumbles ahead of me   catching
erratic feet on the tarmac   ruched
as it is by roots   her left foot sticking
as if in mud   her stoop cranked up
by the pock-marked skin of the drystone wall
she is thrown on   the angle of light   sickish
orange in the early night.   Her mouth
twitches down at the creases   *Bitchy*
Resting Face   though you cannot see it
dark on dark.   You could say she exists
in relief   except there is none   not
for a structure like her   misbuilt   collapsing
inward with each jolt forward. I try
to right her but she will not straighten. The more
I struggle the more she looks broken. She knows
more of pain than your charts can trace
but you will not acknowledge her   hear her. Her name
is a slur. Her body is carrion. It is
too late for this.
                My blood too sticky.
Her edges are blurring.
                        My legs are unravelling.
Her gown of bones is clacking   clacking.
Will we ever reach home?
                        I sink in my clothes
till my breath melts the frost on the empty road.
She pushes ahead of me   carries on walking.
Carries on walking.
                Carries on walking.

Untethering

It began with long yellow light at the hazy
fringes of a place I tumbled into,
leaves underfoot covering up
my knack for not belonging. I was told
to stop the aching, I needed to see myself
sinking into a loamy ground
downreaching – the land would lend me the stability
I lacked. Some years later but back

the wisest woman I've known yet said to me
you'll leave when you're ready.   I can't bear this body
overwintering in another ground, like a cutting,
greening. I am not a tree, my roots
blanketed by rock, my roots tunnelled under
the weight of the lake bed, my roots knotted rock
in the puzzle of a dry stone wall. Unthink
that sinking. Unthink that tether. Take

this light – that sweet, that loving yellow,
the mist erasing the horizon as though
there is nothing beyond the lip of the valley,
its kiss – could anyone turn from it now?

Hope Cove

There is Outer Hope then Inner Hope
depending on how you approach, a steep
clamber between them in either direction.

I'd forgotten how it was then – Hope –
how to get there. The signs were clear
but the roads wound narrow and alien, cornering

blind, and the sun so bright at times
I was shy of moving. And yet we arrived,
the sea where it always was, white

and thrumming, thick with weed. In Outer
Hope we followed our feet, rising
over a bridge of spray and light

from Bigbury Bay to Bolt Tail, Cornwall
a whisper off a ghost-horizon, drowned
out by the wrecking din. You should know,

Hope is a shattered Armada. But some
bright midday you may stand in its centre,
all the thatch-life of Inner Hope fanning

its tail-feathers, spreading its wings, and launching
off from the cob walls in song: disharmonious,
glorious. The earth is red. The air

is salt, and keeps pushing you on, bears you
up over pillars of scrub and rusted
mud through the thin blue brine of the sky

to a bed of brambles and dog-roses, tamarisks.
Now you remember what it looks like, Hope.
Now you remember where it is.

Basic Nest Architecture

for E.H.

You had the dream of drinking tea forever.
I fled from the flooded world. Woke
out of a car. In its rear view mirror
the wave grew taller. You broke yourself,
gave birth. There was a beehive, you said.
I shrank us all down, had us interred
in its chambers, feeding on royal jelly
in peanut-shaped queen cells, bee space freeing
our frames without smashing our cups: grubs
developing queen morphology.

Acknowledgements

Thanks are due to Arts Council England for their financial assistance whilst working towards this collection, and to the New Writing North for granting an extract from it the 2014 Andrew Waterhouse Prize in the Northern Writers Awards. I am ever-grateful for the invaluable guidance offered by many individuals over the years it has taken to bring this collection to print. There are too many of you to name, but particular thanks are due to Eileen Pun, Emily Hasler, Mark Ward and all the Wordsworth Trust regulars for a continual sense of poetic community, and to the wider literary community in Cumbria and Lancashire for their support and encouragement over the last decade. I might not have believed in the positive power of a community of poets if it were not for the wonderful experiences I have had at StAnza over the years, and I must credit Eleanor Livingstone, Brian and Jean Johnstone, and Jim and Lorna Carruth for helping create that environment and making me feel part of it. I am immensely grateful to Carola Luther for her excellent advice at all times; to Éireann Lorsung for her encouragement and for offering an alternative model; to Rebecca Bilkau and all the Beautiful Dragons for their spirit of collaborative adventure; and to Will Smith for his unwavering support. You not only helped create the habitat in which these poems could be written, but helped me believe in them. Thanks also to my editor Amy Wack and the team at Seren for all their expertise and encouragement.

Thanks to everyone who has helped this collection along the way by publishing, commissioning or endorsing individual poems, including: *1110, And Other Poems, Flax, Keats-Shelley Review, Lines Underwater, Magma, Mslexia, New Welsh Reader, Pilot Pocket Book, The Clearing, The Lonely Crowd*, Beautiful Dragons Press and Sidekick Books. 'Waking the Well', 'Dreaming the Organ' and 'Illustrations of Grasmere Church' were written for *Holy Detritus*, an exhibition with the Lakes Art Collective in St. Oswald's, Grasmere. Selections from this book won the 2012 Mslexia Pamphlet Prize and were published by Seren as 'Shadow Dispatches' in 2013.

'Colony Collapse Disorder' won the 2008 Troubadour Coffee House Poetry Prize; 'Sky, Falling' the 2011 Kent Sussex Poetry Prize; and 'A

Short History of the Moon' the 2014 Wigtown Prize. 'Buzz Pollination' was placed joint second in the 2013 Keats Shelley Prize and 'Causeway' second in the 2014 Poets and Players Competition. 'Heron/Snow' was placed third in the 2014 Battered Moons Prize and 'Tiny Glass Horses' third in the 2015 Café Writers Prize.

'Flood Histories' was shortlisted in the 2013 Wells Literature Festival Prize and 'Begin' in the 2015 Fish Poetry Prize. Commendations were received for 'When I Lived Alone' in the 2009 Robert McLellan Competition; 'Kindling' in the 2010 Wigton Prize; 'The Glorious Fellowship of Migraineurs' in the 2010 Troubadour Prize; 'Miracles of Light' in the 2013 William Soutar Prize; 'The Test' in the 2014 Hippocrates Prize; 'Gloria' in the 2015 Ledbury Prize; and 'With Feathers' in the 2016 Magma Editors' Prize.

Notes

'Colony Collapse Disorder' is a term for the sudden devolution of honey bee colonies. 'A short history of the moon' uses information from a local history website, and from *The Plymouth Book of Days* by John Van der Kiste (Stroud: The History Press, 2011).

Athena Glaukopis is an epithet of the Greek goddess, meaning 'bright-eyed'. *Potnia Theron* is an epithet associated with Artemis and variously translated as 'mistress of beasts', or 'our lady of animals'. Dēor is the Old English word which gives us the word 'deer', and denotes any four-footed wild animal, as opposed to domesticated animals.

'Illustrations of Grasmere Church' is found from Mary Armitt's *The Church of Grasmere: A History* (Kendal: Titus Wilson, 1911).

The middle section of 'The Canon of Proportions' is based on Leonardo Da Vinci's notes from Book III of Vitruvius' *De Architectura*, as recorded on his sketch known as Vitruvian Man/The Canon of Proportions.